The following is dedicated to my father, Kermit Vandivier.

I love you and miss you very much Dad! You are always in my thoughts!

On Feb. 19, 1926, Frances Drake Nesbitt was murdered in her Ridge Avenue home in Troy, Ohio. It was a crime which shocked the residents of Troy – then a village of less than 5,000 people – and even today, the crime is still remembered by residents of the time. In terms of the publicity it generates, it was probably one of the most notorious murders in Ohio history, trailing only the Sam Shepard murder case and the Ruppert slayings in Cincinnati. Because of the notoriety, many rumors and half-truths about the case and those connected with it have been circulated. Kermit Vandivier has researched the story over a period of several years, utilizing microfilmed records and newspaper accounts of the day, magazine articles and record of the Cal Crim Detective Agency, and has conducted personal interviews with persons having first-hand knowledge of the crime. The records vary and are often contradictory. The following is based on reasonable examination and evaluation of available information. Some of the conversations and story line have been created to provide continuity. The basic facts, however, are unchanged.

SOMETHING TERRIBLE HAPPENED

"Frances, are you here?"

Mrs. Charles Drake hurried into the living room of her West Canal Street home. Her son-in-law, Jake Nesbitt, was standing just inside the front door.

"Hello, Jake! Are you looking for Frances? She's not here!"

"She's not? She didn't go to work today and I thought maybe she'd spent the evening with you," Nesbitt responded.

Nesbitt and his wife both worked as salespeople for the Kitchen Aid Division of the Hobart Mfg. Co., and although he had gone to work that day, demonstrating the appliances at a food show in Dayton, his wife of 13 months, Frances Nesbitt, also scheduled to work at the show, did not.

"I haven't seen her or talked to her all day. Isn't she at home?" asked Mrs. Drake.

"I don't know. I haven't been home yet. It's almost 10:30 and I just figured she might be here."

"Well, she's not. Why don't you call her? She's probably at home."

Jake went to the telephone and gave "central" his home telephone number. He waited a few minutes then hung up.

"No answer," he said. "She must be visiting some friends. Well, I guess I'll go on home and wait for her to call. She'll probably want me to pick her up somewhere." He told his mother-in-law goodnight and walked out to his car.

A half-hour later, the telephone of Johnson West, a friend and the nearest neighbor of the Nesbitt's, rang. Glancing at the clock, West, who was about to retire for the night, noted the time – 11 o'clock? Who would be calling at this time of night?

Picking up the phone, he recognized the voice of Jake Nesbitt. "Come over quick. Something terrible has happened!"

"What is it, Jake?" West asked. "What's the matter?" "Frances has had an accident. Something terrible has happened to Frances." said Jake.

West recognized the urgency in Nesbitt's voice, and stopping only to put on a coat, he hurried to the Nesbitt home. He opened the door and stepped inside to find Nesbitt pointing to the bathroom door. "In there. It's Frances."

West rushed into the bathroom and stopped just inside the door. The body of Frances Nesbitt, clad only in a thing nightgown, was lying in the partially-filled tub, her feet sticking over the side.

Quickly, West pulled Frances from the tub and tried to revive her. He gave up after a few minutes, rushed to the telephone and called a doctor.

Jake Nesbitt appeared to be in a state of shock and although West, while waiting for the doctor to arrive, attempted to find out what had happened, he could get no coherent response.

Within a few minutes, Dr. L. N. Lindenberger arrived and after a brief examination of Frances, went to the phone and while explaining to "central" what had happened, asked her to call the police, the coroner and the sheriff.

The first to arrive on the scene was Troy Policeman, Michael O'Connor, followed in short order by Chief of Police, John Sharits, Coroner C.J. Hance and Miami County Sheriff, Mont Spillman.

There were soon joined by other law officers and Miami County Prosecutor, L.E. Harvey.

Dr. Lindenberger and Hance complete their preliminary examination of the body and determined that Frances had died of one or more severe blows to the head from a blunt instrument, that she had died sometime between 11 and 12 o'clock, that she had not been killed in the bathtub, and that she had not been wearing the nightgown when she was killed.

The time of death was determined by the fact that the crystal on Frances' wristwatch had been broken when she apparently struggled with her killer and the hands caught on a piece of the broken crystal in the 12 o'clock position. Thus, they theorized she had been killed sometime after 11 and before 12 – whether a.m. or p.m. was unknown.

Her head and her feet were bloody and there were bloodstains on the floor, sink and walls of the bathroom, yet, the white nightgown had no bloodstains on it, although the part which had been in water had been stained pink. They agreed she had either been naked when killed, or wearing another gown.

While the medical authorities were conducting their examination, police officers had been searching the house thoroughly for clues and found blood between the living room and the bedroom. In the bathroom, they found a comb with a few human hairs on it and dried blood between the teeth.

In the bedroom, the found signs of a struggle – a spindle had been broken off a bedpost and a wall clock had been smashed. The clock's hands were stopped at 8:30.

Meanwhile, Harvey, Sharits and Spillman were questioning the shaken Nesbitt about the events of the day.

The night before the tragedy, Nesbitt related, he and Frances had retired late. Nesbitt said he awakened the next morning, went to the basement and stirred up the fire in the coal furnace. Then he went upstairs, shaved and dressed.

He went back to the basement, put more coal on the fire, unlocked the outside basement door, and then went back upstairs.

Then he put on his coat, swept the snow off the front porch and walked across the street to the garage where he and Frances kept their autos.

After backing his car from the garage, he drove across the street and stopped near the basement door. The Nesbitt home was built on a hillside and the basement opened directly to the outside.

He went into the basement where he kept several KitchenAid appliances stored, removed one of them, locked the basement door from the inside, and then went back up the stairs into the house.

Frances was still half-asleep, he told authorities, and he wrote a note telling her to be sure and adjust the furnace drafts before she left the house. He said it was often her custom to go to work after he did, because she occasionally had appointments of her own and even though they did essentially the same work, they did not necessarily always work in the same place at the same time.

He said he told her goodbye, then left the house, leaving the door unlocked.

From there, he went to the Weintrauh's Dog Hose Restaurant where he ate breakfast, then on to the local garage where he bought a key to the trunk of his auto. He told officers this was necessary since he had broken the key and the trunk of the auto was where he kept his merchandise while traveling.

From the garage, he went on to the food show in Dayton, Ohio, not returning until about 10:30 that night, when he went to the Drake home.

After learning the Frances was not at her parent's home, Nesbitt continued, he stopped off at the Dog House again, had a cup of coffee, and then went home.

Arriving at the darkened house, he said, he parked the car in the garage, noticing that Frances' auto was still inside. He walked across the street to his home, tried the front door and found it unlocked, just as he had left it that morning. He went inside and turned on the lights.

He told officers the first thing he noticed after turning on the lights was that the note he left on the table for France that morning was still there. Then, he continued, he noticed the disarray of the house, saw bloodstains and signs of a terrific struggle.

Then he went on through the house to the bathroom – and found Frances.

Nesbitt was questioned and re-questioned for several hours, but each time he related the same sequence of events.

Authorities now began to piece the evidence together. If Frances had not been wearing the nightgown when she was killed, had she been nude or had she been wearing something else?

Nesbitt, upon questioning, said that the night before the murder, she had been wearing a blue dress. But he was sure she had been wearing the gown when she went to bed.

What had he worn to bed? Pajamas.

Where were they? In the hamper where soiled clothing was kept.

Officers made a quick search for the blue dress but couldn't locate it. A pair of man's pajamas was found in the clothes hamper. The "missing" blue dress was found after a second, more thorough search of the clothes closets, and that clue fizzled.

The mystery remained. Frances Nesbitt had almost certainly not been wearing the white gown when she was killed, so what HAD she been wearing, if anything, and where was it?

It was now nearly four a.m. on Saturday morning, and both Nesbitt and the officers on the scene were tired.

Sharits had never conducted a homicide investigation and decided to call the Dayton Police Department for assistance.

Frances' parents had been notified earlier of the tragedy and had told Jake that when police were through questioning him, he was to come to their house to stay.

By this time, it was after 4 a.m. Authorities decided that Nesbitt had been through enough for one day and he was allowed to leave.

The first day of Jake Nesbitt's ordeal was finally over.

ALL OF TROY WAS BUZZING ABOUT THE MURDER ON RIDGE AVENUE

The brutal murder of Frances Drake Nesbitt rocked the village of Troy and shock waves traveled far!

Reporters were at the scene of the crime a few minutes after her body was found in the bathtub of her home and within a few hours, the story was on the news wires of three press services _ United Press, Associated Press and International News Service.

It was Saturday, Feb. 20, 1926, and the Troy Daily News published on Saturday afternoons then. But the people of Troy didn't need the newspaper to inform them about a tragedy. Long before the Troy Daily News – with its two-line banner headline – rolled off the presses, most of the people in town already knew what happened at 1146 Ridge Ave., or thought they did.

Frances Nesbitt was well known in Troy. She was an athletic sort and was considered by some to be a "tomboy."

A 1917 Troy High School graduate, she went from there to Ohio State University where she excelled as an athlete. She was OSU women's tennis champion during three of her four years and she also like to swim and play golf.

Her marriage to Jake Nesbitt in 1925, just 13 months before her death, was considered by some to be a "storybook" marriage. Jake was an orphan and had played football at Troy High School. He and Frances were employed as sales representatives for the KitchenAid Division of Hobart Manufacturing Co.

After their marriage, the Nesbitts often entertained and were seen frequently as various social events. It was natural, then, that when the news of Frances' murder became known, a great many people in Troy were personally interested.

The central switchboards at the telephone company began to light up shortly after 7 o'clock on the Saturday morning after her body was found and by 9 o'clock, every available operator had been called in. In those days, telephone subscribers could call "central" and get such information as the correct time, where the fire trucks were going or who had own last nights' basketball game.

That morning, they were kept busy supplying the details of Frances Nesbitt's murder. Calls came in from all over the county. Some were from former residents who had known the victim, others from the merely curious.

The rumor mills were already going full blast and there were stories about an "insane" killer being on the loose. The police department and Sherriff's office were flooded with phone calls from citizens demanding to know if the killer had been found – and if not, why not? Why isn't somebody doing something?

The late Ray Steinmetz, a long-time employee and former executive editor of the Troy Daily News, recalled that hectic day in an interview several years ago.

"The phones at the Troy Daily News were ringing off the hook. Newspapers from all over the country were calling us. Some wanted more details on the murder than the wire services had given out and others wanted us to "string" (serve as correspondent) for them."

"We had a time getting the paper out that day because of all the phone calls." Steinmetz recalled, "We had at least a dozen calls from reporters wanting to know where Troy was, how to get there and if there was a hotel in town."

Meanwhile, the authorities had been busy. Joseph Wilcox and James Foote, former Dayton detectives who had become private investigators, had been called by the Troy Police Chief, John Sharits, to assist in the investigation.

Sharits had never conducted a murder investigation before, and he needed – and wanted – all the help he could get. Wilcox and Foote arrived at the Nesbitt home early Saturday morning and began to search for evidence.

Troy Police Officers, meanwhile, were checking out Jake Nesbitt's activities of the day before and Coroner C.J. Hance performed an autopsy. By Saturday night, exhausted authorities summed up their findings:

- Hance reported that Frances had been murdered about 12 hours before her body was found; that she had been killed by several blows to the head from a blunt instrument; that she had not been criminally assaulted; that he had found no food in her stomach. The latter fact was to have a bearing on the case, since it would help establish the time of death.
- The fact that her murderer had placed her body in the partially filled bathtub created a problem, since the cold water speed up the onset of rigor mortis and the rigor mortis process is a major factor in the determination of the time of death.
- An electric iron cord and plug had been found, but no iron. There was a possibility that the iron could have been the murder weapon. That clue quickly petered out, however, when Sharits remembered placing the iron in the icebox in the Nesbitt kitchen. (He never explained why he put it there, but it was generally assumed he had done it unconsciously.)
- A white come with blood stains between the teeth had been found in the bathroom.
- The crystal of Frances' wristwatch, which she was wearing at the time of the murder, had been broken and the hands had caught on a piece of the crystal in the 12 o'clock position.
- A fragment of the crystal had been found in the living room, indicating that she had probably struggled with the murderer in that room.

- There were bloodstains in the bedroom, on the bathroom wall, in the toilet and in the sink.
- A clock in the bedroom was broken and it had been stopped at 8:30.
- There were no signs of scratches or injuries to Jake Nesbitt. He had willingly undergone a thorough examination by the police that day.
- Jake Nesbitt's account of the event of the previous day, up to and including the discovery of his wife's body, checked out to the last detail.
- There was one other piece of information that had been learned, but its significance, if any, could not be evaluated. Nesbitt told police that before he left eh house the day before, he had placed his soiled pajamas in the clothes hamper. A pair of pajamas were found in the clothes hamper, but they were cont considered soiled, at least by police. This was arbitrary, however – how soiled is – soiled?

The fact was filed for future reference.

The authorities considered several theories about the murder.

1. A man had entered the house intending to rape Mrs. Nesbitt, but had been warded off by her vicious struggle.
2. Mrs. Nesbitt had surprised a burglar and had been killed by him. Nothing of value had been taken from the house, however, so this theory was not supported by factual evidence.
3. Mrs. Nesbitt had been slain by her husband.

The latter theory was the most sensitive of all, yet it was a definite possibility that had to be considered. Most of the local people involved in the investigation knew the Nesbitts and, like most Trojans, believed that the marriage was "ideal" or nearly so.

Jake's story had been checked out and confirmed, but there was one nagging detail which somehow didn't seem right.

When Jake Nesbitt had discovered his wife's body, he had immediately telephone his friend and neighbor, Johnson West, and told him, "Something terrible has happened. Frances has had an accident."

These were strange words, indeed. Jake had admitted that when he first entered the house, he was aware there had been a struggle. He told of seeing blood on the walls and floors, then finding the body. Obviously, his wife had been brutally murdered: Why "Frances has had an accident."? Why not "Frances is dead" or "Frances has been killed."?

Still, officers reasoned, Jake had certainly been in a state of shock after seeing his wife's body and couldn't really be held responsible for his choice of words, considering the circumstances.

It was now nearly 20 hours since Frances' body had been found and authorities had to admit they were not much nearer to a solution than they were when they first walked into the Nesbitt home the night before.

Meanwhile, the rumors circulating around town became more vicious and Jake Nesbitt was their target. Jake was about to be arrested and charged with the murder. Someone suggested that he get an attorney and see if the rumors couldn't be squelched.

Jake consulted attorney L.H. Shipman and the following day, Sunday, Feb. 21, issued a formal written statement.

In that statement, he said he was "shocked" that anyone could suspect him of the crime and repeated the account of his movements on the day of the murder. He concluded the statement with a plea for assistance from the public, asking anyone with information about the crime to contact him or police.

His attorney, Shipman, issued his own statement, pleading with the public to "Give him (Nesbitt) a chance."

On Monday, three days after her murder, Frances Drake Nesbit was buried. Jake broke down at the funeral and wept.

NO ANSWERS AND PRECIOUS FEW LEADS

By the time Frances Drake Nesbitt was buried on Monday, Feb. 22, 1926, three days after her murder, Troy had already become the focal point, not only of the media, but of the morbidly curious.

The day before, Sunday, dozens of cars made their way past the Nesbitt home at 1146 Ridge Ave. Many of them had out-of-state license plates – Kentucky, Indiana, Michigan and Tennessee.

Not all of the curious had driven especially to Troy to see the home, of course. U.S. 25 9now Co. Rd. 25-A, and in Troy, South Market Street) was a major north-south thoroughfare and many of the travelers using the highway had heard of the tragedy and decided to include a detour past the Nesbitt home (already given the name of "The House of Mystery" by the press) on their itinerary.

Extra police were on duty to handle the traffic and guards had to be posted to ward off souvenir hunters. Fights broke out among persons attempting to catch a glimpse of the bathroom where Frances had been found.

Reports from Dayton, Cincinnati, Indianapolis, Chicago, Toledo, Cleveland, Louisville and Columbus newspapers descended on Troy like a pestilence and quickly found a temporary "office" at the Troy Daily News.

The TDN was located then on West Main Street in the building that once occupied the Flash restaurant, conveniently near the jail, courthouse and police station.

Frances Nesbitt was buried from her parent's home on West Canal Street and newspaper accounts say that "hundreds" of people filed past her casket.

The press had a field day and the sorrowful funeral was wrung of every possible tear as each reporter tried to "out sensationalize" his fellow journalists.

On Wednesday, Feb. 24, a coroner's inquest was conducted. It had originally been announced that the inquest would be closed to both public and press, but those plans had been changed, apparently unknown to the public, and relatively few spectators were on hand.

It was just as well, because almost every available seat was taken by members of the press.

The inquest began as a routine affair, with the coroner presenting his findings and police officers and other person connected with the case fiving testimony, including a Dayton chemist who stated he had examined the stomach of the victim and could find no trace of poison.

The Jake Nesbitt was called to the stand and questioned about events leading up to his discovery of his wife's body. Although most o the story had already become general knowledge, questioning was expanded to include an account of events on Feb. 17, the Wednesday prior to his wife's murder.

They had house guests that night, Jake related, Mr. and Mrs. Prentiss Brown of Columbus. Nesbitt said that since there was only one bed in the house, he had borrowed a cot from Frances' parents, and set it up in the living room of his home. The Browns slept in the Nesbitts' bed, Frances slept n the sofa in the living room and Jake slept on the cot. The next morning, Thursday, the Browns had returned to Columbus.

Two questions put to him by Prosecutor C.J. Harvey were later proved to be crucial.

- What color were the pajamas he word that Wednesday night?

Jake replied that he had worn no pajamas. He explained that the Browns had already retired when he discovered he had forgotten to get his pajamas from the bedroom dresser. Not wanting to disturb his guests, he had slept in his underclothes.

- On Thursday night, the night before the murder, what side of the bed had he slept on?

Jake answered that he had slept on the side next to the wall.

Then, Troy Patrolman Michael O'Connor, who had been the first officer to arrive on the murder scene, stated that he had carefully examined the bloodstained bed and in his opinion, the side of the bed next to the wall had not been slept in.

The spectators gasped and reporters scribbled furiously in their notebooks. This was the first apparent discrepancy in Jake Nesbitt's version of events.

The people in the courtroom undoubtedly expected further startling developments – especially concerning the question of what Jake had worn to bed two nights prior to the slaying – but they were disappointed.

The inquest was concluded late that night with Coroner C.J. Hance announcing that a ruling would be delayed until after he had time to assess all the testimony and evidence.

It was not until three days later that Hance officially ruled Frances Nesbitt's death was due to blows on the head, delivered by "an unknown weapon at the hands of an unknown person."

In the meantime, detectives had questioned the Browns about their visit, with special emphasis on what Jake had worn to bed.

Both stated he had worn blue pajamas, a fact they remembered well because Jake, himself, had pointed out that the pajamas clashed with his red bathrobe.

Nesbitt emphatically denied the Browns' claim, stating they must be mistaken.

He stated he only had one pair of pajamas – white – and that on the morning he had last seen his wife, he had, after dressing for work, hung them on the back of the bathroom door. (Some accounts had him placing them in the clothes hamper.)

Officers had found the pajamas but they didn't appear to have been worn. In fact, they appeared as though they had been freshly ironed.

Jake explained this by saying he had only worn them the one night, reminding them that he had worn no pajamas the night of the Browns' visit, despite statements by the Browns to the contrary.

As the investigation dragged on, Jake remembered something he had forgotten to tell officers before. He had bought an axe not too long before the murder, an axe that was now missing. Could this be the murder weapon?

A thorough search was made for the axe, but it was never found.

By this time, the investigation ha bogged down and officers re-examined the evidence they had accumulated.

They had assumed that Frances had been murdered sometime between 11 o'clock and noon on Friday, Feb. 19, since the hands on her wristwatch had stopped in the 12 o'clock position. Were they barking up the wrong tree? Had Frances actually been murdered on Thursday night?

The coroner had admitted difficulty in establishing the time of death since Frances' body had been placed in the partially-filled tub of water, disturbing the rigor mortis process.

And despite Jake's statement, detectives believed only one person had slept in the bed that Thursday night. Was it possible that the murder occurred between 11 p.m. and 12 midnight that night, instead of between 11 o'clock and noon the next day?

Hearing of this new theory, Nesbitt and his attorney, L.H. Shipman, conducted their own investigation, intending to prove that Frances was alive when Jake had left for work, just as he had stated.

They questioned several person who had been at the Dayton food show where both Jake and Frances had been working the night before the murder, and found one woman who said she had seen Frances eating popcorn about 10 p.m.

Shipman quickly brought this new evidence to police. The coroner had indicated no food was found in Frances's stomach and since it takes food from seven to ten house to undergo the digestive process, it appeared to substantiate Nesbitt's story that Frances HAD been alive when Jake had left for work.

This, said Shipman, discounted any possibility that Frances had been killed shortly after she and Jake returned home on Thursday night.

But, other discrepancies began to crop up. Jake had said that after leaving the house on the morning of his wife's murder, he had driven to a local garage and bought a key to the trunk of his auto, since he had lost his. This was confirmed by the garage.

Officers making another search of the Nesbitt home, however, found a key to the auto's trunk in the house. The furnace was again examined and this time, a portion of cord, believed to be from pajamas, was found.

Private detectives Joseph Wilcox and James Foote had turned up much of the evidence obtained so far, but admitted they had about reached the limits of their abilities.

By this time, the citizens of Troy were up in arms. Some two weeks had passed and the murder still hadn't been solved.

Then Frances' parents, Mr. and Mrs. Charles Drake, made a dramatic announcement. They weren't at all satisfied with the progress – or rather lack of progress – of the investigating and offered to hire and investigator of their own. The man the proposed to hire was former Dayton Police Chief, James Woodward. Woodward had already conferred with the Drakes and told reporters he had important information about the murder.

Hire him if you want to, retorted authorities, but he can't see any of the evidence we already have and we won't cooperate with him.

Sheriff Mont Spillman toned down this seemingly-hostile attitude by explaining that Wilcox and Foote had both been dismissed from the Dayton police force while Woodward was chief, and they bore a certain amount of resentment against him.

Then, after a long conference with two executives of the Hobart Manufacturing Co. (the parent firm of KitchenAid, the firm for which the Nesbitts work) authorities further retreated and said that they would cooperated with any private detected the Drakes wanted to hire – provide it wasn't Woodward.

Some substantial citizens of the community, headed by Troy Mayor George Stokes, then offered to form a committee to solicit public funds with which to hire an additional private investigator.

Some funds were raised and the committee agreed to hire a detective from the Crim-Ryan Detective Agency, a nationwide firm with a branch office in Cincinnati.

The detective Crim-Ryan assigned to the case was Ora Slater.

The newspapers (and even some of his contemporaries) often referred to Ora Slater ad "Sherlock Holmes." It was an exaggeration – but not much.

Formerly the Sheriff of Hancock County, Indiana, Slater had also served for a number of years on the Cincinnati police force as a detective. Retiring from that job, he joined Crim-Ryan.

An easy-going person in his 50's, Slater was described as a "not-stop talker" who had a natural talent for making friends, even of those who might normally consider him an enemy.

Slater wasn't, of necessity, interested in the physical evidence of crimes, but was more interested in the psychological aspects, such as the whom? And why?

He had made a considerable reputation for himself by solving some seemingly "unsolvable" crimes, crimes which had stumped other sleuths, hence the nickname of "Sherlock Holmes."

For two days following his arrival in Troy, Slater conducted an examination of the Nesbitt home, studied the physical evidence already obtained by other detectives and pondered over the statements of Nesbitt and others connected with the crim.

His conclusion - Jake Nesbitt was guilty.

His job was to prove it.

THE NESBITT MURDER SOLVED ... OR WAS IT?

Ora Slater was described as a "marathon talker with a mouthful of gold teeth>:

In his late fifties, he had a long and distinguished career in law enforcement, having served as an Indian sheriff, a parole official and a detective n the Cincinnati police department, before becoming a top investigator for the Crim-Ryan Private Detective Agency.

His chief asset was his ability to gain the confidence of just about anyone he cared to.

A group of private citizens hired Slater to solve the murder of Frances Nesbitt, 12 days after her body was found in the bathtub of her Ridge Avenue home. Tow private detectives had already been brought into the case, but outside of gathering some flimsy, highly-circumstantial evidence, little progress had been made and authorities were no nearer a solution than they were on the day of the murder.

They were all but certain that she had been killed by her husband of 13 months, Jake Nesbitt, but they needed more substantial evidence – or a confession.

Slater was the man they hoped could get that confession for them.

He spent his first two days on the job interviewing the scant evidence and conducting his own search of the Nesbitt home. His conclusions were the same as his fellow detectives: Jake Nesbitt was guilty but there was simply not enough evidence to bring charges against him.

For the next several days, Slater spent most of his time with Nesbitt, assuring him that he believed in Jake's innocence and was going to try to find the real killer.

Slater and Nesbitt drove around the state, checking out various stories and "tips" which had been received and talking with officers in other cities where murders had recently been committed.

Maybe, just maybe, Slater told Nesbitt, there would be some similarity in the crimes, something which might tie in with the murder of Frances Nesbitt.

On one such trip, they even stayed overnight in Canton, sharing a hotel room.

During those days they exchanged stores of their family lives and it wasn't long before Jake was convinced Ora Slater was his friend, a person he could trust. He was soon to find out differently.

On March 11, nearly three weeks after the murder, Slater met with Sheriff Mont Spillman, Police Chief John Sharits, Prosecutor L. E. Harvey, Special Prosecutor Alva Campbell and Troy Mayor George Stokes.

He had found absolutely no new evidence, he said, and it was highly unlikely that any would be found.

But, he said, he was convinced he could get Jake to confess by confronting him with all the evidence which had been gathered.

The assembled authorities agreed that Slater's suggestion was their only hope and gave their approval.

First, however, they imposed a most unusual condition. Slater could proceed, they said, but only after the evidence was first disclosed to officials of the Hobart Manufacturing Co., the Nesbitts's employer.

The following morning, H. L. Johnston, V.P. of the firm and C.C. Willard, another Hobart official, were called in and Prosecutor Harvey made a full disclosure of all the evidence, including police reports, witnesses' statements and lab reports.

That afternoon, Friday, March 12, exactly three weeks after Frances Drake Nesbitt's death, Slater called on Jake Nesbitt at the home of his in-laws, Mr. and Mrs. Charles Drake, where Jake had been staying since the murder of his wife.

Slater asked Nesbitt to accompany him to the murder scene, adding that "the play is over."

At the Nesbitt home, Jake found two familiar faces – Johnston's and Willard's. Slater explained to Nesbitt that Johnston and Willard were present only as witnesses, to assure Jake that there would be no third degree, no pressure.

The questioning began at 1:30 and for five hours, Slater grilled Nesbitt about his wife's death, asking him over and over to repeat the story he had told police about finding his wife's body.

Slater later said he told Nesbitt that he, Slater, had done all he could for Jake and that if he made a full confession immediately, he, Slater, would call the prosecutor and walk out of the case.

Slater's words apparently had the desired effect, for at 6:30, Jake Nesbitt said, "Don't call now. If you leave Frances out of this, I will tell the truth. I only wish I was with her. I did it. I killed her."

What followed then was a glimpse into the private lives of Jake and Frances Nesbitt.

Jake told of months of bickering, almost since their marriage 13 months before. The bickering was primarily over Frances' job selling KitchenAid appliances. She and her husband had formed a sort of business partnership to sell the appliances and she was far more successful at it then he was.

And, Jake told Slater, Frances never let him forget it. She often urged him to get another job, reminding him that it was the money she earned which paid most of the bills. On Thursday, February 18, the eve of the murder, they had both returned home late from a food show in Dayton.

They were both in an ill mood, said Jake, and a long argument ensued. Frances finally went to bed, while Jake slept on a couch in the living room.

The next morning, Jake continues, he got up as usual and went to the basement to fire the furnace. The furnace began to smoke and Frances, who was awake, called out some cutting remark. He retorted and when he got upstairs, the previous night's argument bloomed anew.

Finally, Jake said, she made some rather disparaging remarks about his relatives and slapped him. He slapped her back and she slapped him once again.

Then, Nesbitt related, he "saw red." There was a struggle and Jake said he remembered choking her. He said he didn't remember hitting her, but did recall seeing a piece of firewood. He also recalled carrying her into the bathroom and remembered taking off his blood-stained pajamas and burning them in the furnace.

He said that sometime during the struggle, Frances said, "Oh, Jake! Don't you love me?"

Jake told Slater, "I remember saying afterward (after killing her) "Oh, God, what have I done?"

Nesbitt said that after the murder, he dressed and left the house. He ate breakfast at the Dog House Restaurant, ran some personal errands, and then went on to the food show in Dayton. That night, as he had already told officers three weeks before, he returned to Troy where he subsequently "discovered" his wife's body.

The news of Nesbitt's confession was not long in reaching the people of Troy. The Troy Daily News had an "extra" on the street within an hour, even before Jake was in jail.

The next day, he was arraigned on a charge of first-degree murder. He pleaded innocent and was bound over to the grand jury, without bond.

On May 11, he was indicted by the Miami County grand jury on a charge of second-degree murder. Trial was set for May 24, but on May 19, Jake Nesbitt, through his attorney, L. H. Shipman, asked for permission to appear in court. Once there, he announced he wanted to plead guilty as charged, explaining that he did not want to put his friends or Frances' family through the ordeal of the trial.

He was immediately sentenced to life imprisonment and on the following day, he was taken to the Ohio State Penitentiary in Columbus.

As prisoner number 55682, Jake Nesbitt soon adapted to prison life and before long, he was a trusty, often serving as chauffeur for the warden.

He was permitted to visit downtown Columbus, unguarded, and was often seen on the streets by acquaintances.

On Jan. 10, 1935, after serving a little less than nine years of his "life" term, Jake Nesbitt was pardoned.

He virtually disappeared on March 31, 1954.

On that day, in the Cincinnati suburb of Oakley, a man and his wife were driving along a quiet street when the car suddenly careened into a pole; its driver slumped over the wheel. Jake Nesbitt was dead.

Cincinnati newspapers carried his death as a routine item until a sharp-eyes editor recognized the name. Reporters descended on the Nesbitt home in Hyde Park, another suburb, hoping to discover how Nesbitt had spent the previous 19 years.

What they found was a widow with two young sons, a widow who was totally unaware of her husband's past!

Beatrice Nesbitt was shocked when she heard the story of Frances Nesbitt. She told reporters she had known nothing of the existence of Jake's first wife. She said Jake once told her he had "made one mistake", but added she had never pressed him for details.

They had met some years earlier and married. She had one son by a previous marriage, whom Jake adopted, and she and Jake had a son of their own.

Reporters soon learned that when Jake left prison, he operated a trucking company for a time, and then worked as a manager of a Kroger Store in Cincinnati. He later opened a delicatessen and carryout in O'Bryonville, a business he and his wife operated until his death.

His neighbors and friends in the community were astounded at the story of the death of Frances Nesbitt, and many refused to believe Nesbitt could have been a murderer.

On April 3, 1954, Jake Nesbitt was buried in Spring Grove Cemetery.

Beatrice Nesbitt created something of a stir later by announcing that she had new information which would clear her husband's name.

But nothing ever care of it and eventually, she, too, virtually dropped from sight, just as Jake had done nearly 20 years before.

For all practical purposes, the case of "The body in the bathtub" – as some newspapers termed it – was closed.

But was it?

THE FINAL CHAPTER OF A BAFFLING MURDER MYSTERY

The mystery surrounding the murder of Frances Drake Nesbitt did not end with a dramatic confession of her husband, Jake Nesbitt.

There have always been rumors of a "cover-up," that Jake "took the rap" for the real murderer. And, those rumors usually contain veiled references to one or more "big shots" at Hobart Manufacturing Co.

Long before her murder, tongues were wagging about Frances Nesbitt, alleging she was "running around on Jake," maintaining one or more extra-marital affairs with some of her superiors at Hobart.

Where or not that gossip was true is anyone's guess. But, it's easy to understand why such gossip would exist.

Frances was an unusual woman for her time. Fairly attractive, out-going and vivacious but she was not very well liked by her female contemporaries. They remember her as an aggressive person – "pushy" – accustomed to getting her own way.

She smoked and she drank – although apparently not to excess – something which even in the "Roaring Twenties" would lead may people to consider her "fast." (In conservative Troy, the Twenties did not roar, they merely groaned.)

She wore her hair short, long before short hair became stylish, and while she was very careful about her appearance, she was not at all "clothes-conscious." For example, she wore the same dress on all the three of the days prior to her murder, something not many women would do even in today's casual times.

But, most important, in those days when women who worked usually held "ladylike" positions as typists or secretaries. Frances Nesbitt was a sales rep – something then considered to be a "man's job."

Her work required her to meet and associate with a number of men and at times, she very likely had to entertain them with dinner and drinks, creating good will and stimulating sales.

She was good at her work and usually excelled her male co-workers in sales. She was always a better salesperson than Jake, a fact she never let him forget and one which he always resented.

And, she ruled their home at 1146 Ridge Ave. "She wore the pants in that family." remarked one lady who remembers Frances. "Not very many people liked her. She was too bossy. She ran Jake's life and he let her get away with it. She knew there was a lot of gossip about her, but it didn't bother her at all. She didn't care. She said "Let them think what they want to." She just didn't care."

It was natural then, that when she was murdered, some Hobart employees were suspected of the crime; if not by police, then certainly by the public and certain circumstances WERE highly suspicious.

For example, in his original statement to police, Jake Nesbitt said that, after finding Frances' body in the partially-filled bathtub, the first person he called was Johnson West, a neighbor who also happened to be Hobart's attorney.

Jake later said he first called a doctor, then told the "central" operator to call police (He also said he did not remember if he had told "central" his address or not.)

Jake then called West, telling him "Something terrible has happened. Frances has had an accident." (Why did he call West and why did he use that particular choice of words? His wife had obviously been murdered – why didn't he say so?)

Johnson West said he called the police and the doctor before going to the Nesbitt home. Asked why he called police, West said he could tell by Nesbitt's voice that something was wrong.

Jake and West both stated that after West arrived at the Nesbitt home, he, West, advised Jake to call a doctor and "you'd better call John Spencer."

Spencer was a sales manager at Hobart. Mfg. and both Jake's and Frances' immediate superior.

Jake called him and Spencer arrived at the Nesbitt home a few minutes later. He, West and Jake engaged in a lengthy conversation. What they said, no one knows.

A couple of days after the murder, a rumor was circulated that Hobart was going to offer a reward for the capture of Frances' killer.

Hobart officials quickly denied the rumor, issuing a prim statement to the effect that it would not be seemly for a private company to become involved with police matters.

There was apparently a change of heart, because within a few days, Hobart Mfg. was not only involved, but two high-ranking officials, H. L. Johnston and C.C. Willard, were, in effect, advising officials about how to conduct the murder investigation.

It was only after consulting with Johnston and Willard that authorities decided to call in private investigator Ora Slater.

But the most shocking developments, at least as far as the involvement of Hobart in the investigation, were:

The admission by Prosecutor L.E. Harvey that he had shown Johnston and Willard all the evidence and testimony that had been gathered during the

investigation. Such action had no legal precedence (Harvey's own words) and was considered by some lawyers then – and most lawyers now – to be highly improper.

And the presence of Johnston and Willard during the final questioning of Nesbitt when he confessed to his wife's murder.

Harvey told the press Johnson and Willard were there only so Nesbitt would have "friends" present o reassure him that he would not be given the third degree.

Harvey repeatedly used the word "friends" in describing the relationship between Johnston, Willard and Nesbitt. Yet there is nothing to suggest that the relationship was anything more than employer-employee. It seems highly unlikely that a mere salesman could be called the "friend" of two high-ranking company officials.

And, if Harvey wanted to reassure Jake that there would be no third degree, why didn't he have Jake's attorney present?

But it wasn't only the unusual interest taken by Hobart officials that triggered widespread rumors of a cover-up.

The entire investigation, from beginning to end, was extremely suspicious and the evidence just doesn't fit in with Jakes' confession.

ITEM: Jake said he killed Frances around 7 o'clock in the morning. Yet the hands of Frances' shattered wristwatch, which was still on her wrist when she was found, were stopped in the 12 o'clock position by a fragment of the broken crystal.

Coroner G.J. Hance ruled that when he arrived at the Nesbitt home, around 11:30 on the night of the murder, Frances had been dead about 10-12 hours. This ruling fits in nicely with the broken watch, but it doesn't jive with Jake's confession.

ITEM: Johnson West stated he and Jake pulled Frances from the bathtub and that he and West threw water on her in an attempt to revive her.

Several area undertakers question this. They generally agree that if Frances had been dead since 7 o'clock or even only since noon, her body would have been in deep rigor and as one undertaker said, "A person would have to be blind not to see that she was dead. I can't imagine anyone trying to revive her."

ITEM: Frances's face and feet were smeared with blood. The bathroom floor and the sink were heavily bloodstained and the bathroom stool was literally filled with blood. Yet, the thin white gown on Frances' body was not stained. It was tinted pink from the blood in the water, but the tint did not extend above the waterline on her gown.

This led authorities to believe that she had either been nude when she was slain or wearing another garment. For days, officers searched for the blue dress Frances had worn the three previous days. It was finally found almost a week later, hanging in the bedroom closet, a closet that had been searched repeatedly before.

Jake Nesbitt said Frances was wearing a nightgown when he killed her and after his confession, no one brought up the subject of the stained gown again.

ITEM: Frances apparently put up a terrific struggle with her murdered, from the living room where she was first struck, through the bedroom and on into the bathroom.

Jake Nesbitt's body was examined by a doctor and police. There wasn't a mark on him.

Jake later offered an explanation. "Frances wasn't very strong in her arms."

Frances Nesbitt, three times OSU women's tennis champion. Frances Nesbitt, who loved to play golf and swim, wasn't strong in her arms?

ITEM: Jake Nesbitt knew almost from the start that he was a prime suspect in his wife's murder. Two days after her death, he retained L.H. Shipman, his attorney.

For the next two weeks, Shipman, who was considered the expert attorney, was with Jake almost constantly and most of Nesbitt's comments were made through him.

Then, Shipman's interest seemed to wane and when Ora Slater came into the case, Shipman allowed his client to travel around the state with him – the man hired to expose the murderer.

Shipman was not present when Nesbitt confessed and he didn't challenge the confession later.

ITEM: Frances' parents, Mr. and Mrs. Charles Drake, firmly believed in Jake's innocence. Mrs. Drake chided police for what she called their "one-track investigation" and offered to hire a private detective on their own. James Woodward, who claimed he had personal knowledge of the case which would shed new light on the murder.

Officials said she could hire Woodward if she wanted, but they would not cooperate with him or show him any evidence already obtained. They said that they didn't believe the two private detectives already brought into the case would cooperate with Woodward because there was some "hard feelings."

They never bothered to ask Woodward what personal information he possessed.

ITEM: Four neighbors of the Nesbitts testified that a red Ford coupe was parked in front of the Nesbitt home most of the day of the murder.

Police searched for the red Ford for several days without success. When Jake confessed, the red Ford was forgotten. No one ever mentioned it again.

ITEM: A Troy Daily News carrier boy told police he went to the Nesbitt home late in the afternoon on the day of the murder. He said he found the door standing "wide open." There were no lights on in the house (it was dusk) and no one answered his knock. He tossed the paper inside the house and left. He didn't close the door.

Jake told police that after he killed Frances, he left the house, shutting the door behind him. He said when he returned home that night, the door was closed and the evening paper way lying on the front porch.

ITEM: Jake Nesbitt had no money with which to pay an attorney and the court appointed Shipman to represent him during his trial. (Prior to that appointment, Shipman represented Nesbitt on a no-fee basis)>

Yet, in 1935, when Jake was pardoned – during the very depths of the Great Depression – he had enough money to open his own trucking business, and later, a deli and carryout.

There are many other items – the missing axe, the lost murder weapon, etc. – which cannot be explained, especially at this late date. But they all indicate that they investigation into Frances Nesbitt's murder was not only totally incomplete, but grossly mishandled.

Who really killed Frances Drake Nesbitt?

It had to be Jake.

He almost got away with it, but the missing pajamas trapped him. Or rather, the lie he told about the pajamas.

Jake told police the only pajamas that he owned were the freshly-ironed white ones they found hanging on the bathroom door.

Yet, Mr. and Mrs. Prentiss Brown, college friends of the Nesbitts, who had stayed overnight with them two days prior to Frances's murder, testified – and they had no reason to lie – that on that night, Jake had on blue pajamas and that he had even remarked about how they clashed with his red robe.

Jake swore he owned no blue pajamas and that the Browns must either be mistaken or lying: and that did him in.

Even so, had he not confessed, he probably would never have been convicted.

Attorneys, judges and police today say there was simply not enough evidence to convict him and that if he hadn't pleaded guilty, he probably would not have been brought to trial.

The lie about the pajamas was certainly damaging, but it was not evidence. Ora Slater claimed he found a piece of pajama cord in the furnace, but even if he did, there was nothing to link the cord with the missing pajamas.

When Jake confessed, his words were, "If you will leave Frances out of this, I will tell the truth."

Leave Frances out of what? She was already dead. What did Jake want Ora Slater to leave Frances out of?

No one knows, or likely ever will. All the principals in the case are dead and their secrets died with them.

Only the "House of Mystery", as newspapers called the Nesbitt home on Ridge Avenue, still remains.

Not on Ridge Avenue, however.

A year after Jake Nesbitt entered prison, the house was moved. It sits now on the quiet side street in Troy, not too far from its original location.

The outside has been remodeled and the interior has been decorated and changed many times over.

It's very possible that its' present occupants aren't even aware that they are living in the house, where, on a cold, snowy February morning more than a half-century ago, something terrible happened to Frances.

(The following article, written by my Dad, appeared the same day as the final chapter of the Nesbitt article.)

LOOKING AROUND by Kermit Vandivier

I moved to Troy in 1963 and I hadn't been in town more than a month or so when I first heard about the 1926 Nesbitt murder.

It intrigued me, not only because of the controversy surrounding it, but because 1926 was the year I was born.

I didn't believe all the rumors about a "cover-up" or about "Hobart big shots" being involved because such rumors generally crop up in cases like the Nesbitt murder.

I began serious research on the murder about five years ago, intending to squelch, once and for all, the ugly rumors.

It didn't take long, however, to realize that there was something to the rumors after all, that there HAD been a cover-up.

As I read accounts of the murder in the Troy Daily News, it became more and more obvious that tremendous pressure had been put on authorities by someone, and pressure had been put on the Troy Daily News, as well.

It has generally been thought that out-of-town newspaper reporters who descended on Troy grossly exaggerated – sensationalized – certain aspects of the case.

Some of them probably did, but it's difficult to believe that every reporter from every paper was guilty of sensationalism.

The New York Times, hardly a paper known for sensationalism, carried the story on its pages, and even published it in its Paris edition.

Generally, those stories concerned the alleged interference of Hobart Mfg. Co. officials in the investigation.

The Troy Daily News hotly denied such interference and called upon Trojans to rally around the flag and put such rumors to rest.

It personally too on – editorially – some of the Cleveland newspapers, blasting them for fomenting rumors and printings "half-truths."

The TDN, however, was itself guilty not only of printing half-truths, but of deliberately printing misleading information.

A classic example is its story of the inquest. The TDN dismissed the inquest as a "routine affair," specifically stating, not once but several times, that nothing of significance was revealed at the inquest. It stated that the only "surprising testimony" was the revelation that the coroner had sent Frances Nesbitt's stomach to a Dayton chemist for analysis.

As a matter of fact, the most startling testimony at the inquest was Jakes' testimony about the missing pajamas.

After Jakes' confession some two weeks later, the Ten blandly reported Jake's inquest testimony about the pajamas, commenting that "of course" the missing pajamas were the most significant factor in the case.

Long before Jake's indictment, a Cleveland reporter wrote that there was a cover-up under way – engineered by a "group of rich persons" - and that the prosecutor was going to arrange for a grand jury indictment on second-degree murder, Jake would plead guilty before the case came to trial.

The TDN jumped on the reporter with both feet, accusing him of sensationalism and of impugning the reputation of some of Troy's finest citizens.

What actually happened is, of course, history. Jake was indicted on second-degree murder charges and he did plead guilty before the trial.

I believe there was a cover-up, but I don't believe Jake Nesbitt "took the rap" for anyone.

I believe the cover-up involved the circumstances around Frances' murder, and I don't't' believe the murder happened the way Jake said it did.

Jake and Frances may have argued about things, but the argument that resulted in her murder had to be about her extra-curricular activities.

Why else would Jake say, "If you leave Frances out of this, I'll tell you everything"?

It's rather obvious that Ora Slater was brought into the case, not to solve the murder, but to negotiate with Jake Nesbitt.

Slater did not turn up one shred of tangible, meaningful evidence and the time he spent with Jake ostensibly trying to "size him up" was actually used to feel Jake out, to find out just what he knew about Frances and her affairs, and most important, to find out what Jake intended to do about it.

Jake knew he was a prime suspect and so did his attorney. But they both also know that the evidence against Jake was entirely circumstantial, that is was highly unlikely he would ever be convicted if brought to trial.

There is only one logical explanation for his confession. There is only one logical explanation for his easy life in the penitentiary. There is only one logical explanation for the fact that he was pardoned or that he came out of prison an affluent man with enough money to open his own trucking line.

Jake had a price and someone paid it.

The following items were gathered by my Dad during his "investigation" of the Frances Drake Nesbitt murder....

The clearing up of the murder case failed to stop the flow of visiting motorist here, tags on the machines showing them come from distant states to get view of the murder scene.

Sunday machines were parked solid along Ridge Avenue with swarms of people going over the wrecked foundation and inspecting he cellar over which the home formally stood. The curious were also peering behind and through the cracks in the boards that were over the windows, as the little bungalow stood on the wrecking truck in the roadway. Many found the cellar door open and this called for a crusade into the murder home itself, until the officers were called and put a stop to entering the building.

One attorney, who claims to have had an extended interview with Nesbitt before he pleaded guilty and before his trip to the penitentiary, said that he is positive that Nesbitt killed his wife with an axe which the officials have failed to locate. He says that, according to Nesbitt's own statement, that during the fatal quarrel, his wife went to the cellar and brought the axe up herself. This was supposed to have been during the "red rage" when he seized the weapon from his wife and struck the fatal blow. It is also said, according to the attorney, that the murdered disposed of the axe on his way to Dayton, on the morning of February, 20, when he dropped it in the Miami River at the north edge of the city.

Nesbitt's easy life at the penitentiary, where Judge W.D. Jones sentenced the slayer for life at hard labor, has also aroused the citizens of this city. Recently, a chicken thief was sentenced to the same prison for five to fifteen years and the statements on the streets could be heard, "Well the chicken thief will be in the pen longer than Nesbit." Others have been heard to say, "It looks like it is more popular to kill you wife than to steal chickens."

Troy citizens know that Nesbitt is being shown many privileges at the Columbus prison. According to letters received form Nesbitt, he has already been allowed to take trips to the business district, unaccompanied by guards. He is living in what is called a large airy dorm instead of a little, dungy prison cell and is being given instructions in X-ray work.

THE FOLLOWING IS THE STATEMENT OF JACOB NESBITT:

"It comes as a shock to me that I am suspected of the murder of my wife. Following numerous rumors up the streets that such was the case, and I was about to be arrested, or put through some sort of examination, I, upon advice of friends, employed L.H. Shipman, of Troy, as my counsel."

"I desire to make a statement of all I know of the death of my wife, in the hope that it may result in the discovery of the person guilty of this crime."

"My wife and I were married January 24, 1925. We have never had any domestic trouble of any kind. She had my fullest confidence, and I believe I had hers."

"We were both employed by the Kitchen Aid Company, of Troy, as salesmen, selling a device known at "KitchenAid."

"On Wednesday evening, February 17, we had some company at our house. A young man and his wife, Mr. and Mrs. Prentice Brown, of Columbus. We did not have sufficient beds, and we borrowed a sanitary cot of Mrs. Charles Drake, who is the mother of my wife. We also borrowed some bed clothing. They stayed with us Wednesday night."

"Thursday morning, we had breakfast around about eight o'clock, and I went on to Dayton in my Ford by myself, arriving there sometime between nine and ten o'clock."

"I called on some prospects in the morning. My wife came down later on a bus, and she came over to the food show, where I was in charge of the KitchenAid display about the middle of the afternoon. My wife stated at the food show most of the afternoon and I went over to the store of the Estate Household Appliance Company, where we have the KitchenAid display. We had our evening meal together, and we went back to the food show and stayed there a little while and then my wife went to Keith's by herself. She came back from the show to the food display, and shortly after this, we came home together in the Ford coupe which I had driven down to Dayton in the morning."

"On the way home, she told me about having seen some Troy boys with their girls at the show. All the way home, she was in good humor, and as it was foggy and rainy, we came home rather slowly, and the latter part of the journey, she seemed to become drowsy."

"I drove up in front of the house and let her out, gave her the key, and she went on into the house by herself."

"I drove on across the street and put the car in the garage where it is usually kept. I came back to the house and found her sitting in the big chair, reading. I went down and fixed the furnace, sat and read a little while, smoke a pipe, and then she prepared for bed and retired first, and in a few minutes, I followed her and we slept together in the bed in the bedroom. Nothing happened during the night at all. I heard no noise and we both slept soundly."

"On the morning of Friday, the 19th, I got up about seven o'clock, closed our windows, went down to the furnace, and put in some coal. The fire was low, and I did not put in the very much coal. I then went to the bathroom and shaved. Then I dressed."

"I then went back to the furnace, and put in some more coal, after the first coal had started to burn, and I unlocked the outside door of the basement as I could get out a KitchenAid later. I then went back to the bathroom and put some talcum on my face, and then went to my wife, where she was lying in bed, and kissed her goodbye and then swept the snow off the porch and walk."

"I then went across the street to a garage where I kept my Ford coupe and drove it in front of the house. Then, I went to the house and carried out one KitchenAid and a box of attachments, and put them in my car. I then locked the basement door and went back up through the house. I also had some new cookbooks which the company furnished to users of KitchenAid. I had some of these along with me. My wife, being about half asleep, I wrote her a note before I left the house, to close damper in furnace, and to get some money off Mr. Spencer."

"I drove down town and did some errands and got something to eat at Weirauch's Restaurant."

"From there, I drove to Dayton to the store of the Estate Household Appliance Company, where we have a display of KitchenAid. I left my car out in the alley, back of the store, and took the KitchenAid and the accessories into the store. At this place in the morning, I saw Henry Langenburg, who is the manager of the store."

"After this, I had some prospects in Dayton, and I called at about four homes, one of them was Mrs. Charles Bieser, there I showed the chef how to work their KitchenAid and talked with Mrs. Bieser. These calls took all morning."

"At noon, I returned to the store and took lunch at the First Street Branch of the Y.W., then went back to the store and probably at about one o'clock, I went to the KitchenAid display at the food show at Memorial Hall. I was there all afternoon until about 5:20 p.m. I got my evening meal at the same cafeteria of the Y.W., and went back to the food show, and was around there until I left for home around about 10:30 p.m."

"I had expected my wife to come to Dayton and be in the store in the afternoon while I was at the food show. At 5:30, when I came back, I found that she was not there, but I thought nothing of this, because she frequently would get prospects and changer her plans."

"I came home to Troy, arriving after 11 o'clock. I went first to the home of my wife's mother. Went in the house and called my wife's name and her mother answered, saying that Frances was not there. I asked where she had been there to lunch and she said no."

"Then she said "Call up out home." I did so and received no answer. I started for home, and on the way, stopped at Weirauch's and got a cup of coffee and drove out to the house and saw it was dark. I assumed that she was at some friends and expected to find a note telling me where to go after her, and I left my car out in front with the lights burning, got the mail out of the mail box and went up on the porch, and hunted for ht key where it is usually kept and it was not there."

"I tried the door and it was unlocked. I turned on the lights and went to the desk where she usually placed notes for me and found no note and then say blood on the floor. I hurried into the bedroom, turned on the light and saw more blood on the floor and then went into the adjoining bathroom, turned on the light and say her lying in the tub."

"I took her by the arm and found it was cold and clammy and the horror and shock was such that I hardly knew what to do next, but I ran to the telephone and called exchange and told her to call the Police department first and then asked the telephone operator to get me Dr. L.N. Lindenberger. I talked with Dr. Lindenberger and told him to come out at once, that something terrible had happened."

"I then asked the operator to get our friend, Johnson West, and told him to come over right away. I then called Mother Drake. I then went back to the bathroom and saw the mass of blood in the toilet and then went on the porch, I heard Johnson West's door slam in a moment Johnson West came p the steps to the porch. He went in the house and I followed. Mr. West lifted up the body partly out of the tub. I turned on the water and washed my wife's face. He then told me to call Mr. Spencer by phone, which I did; a lot of people came in."

"I don't remember much about the details after this, excepting that after some hours, I went to my wife's mother's home, where I have been most of the time until the funeral today."

The very first statement from Jacob Nesbitt read as follows:

"I am at a lost to know who committed the crime. I trust and hope that the matter will soon be solved and especially request that anyone having any information of any kind which would lead to a solution will be willing to give all the assistance possible."

SECOND WIFE

SHOCKED BY THE NEWS

HER LATE HUSBAND KILLED FIRST SPOUSE—1926 MURDER FAMOUS

Jacob C. Nesbitt, 55, 3347 Potomac Ave., Hyde Park, who died Wednesday at the wheel of his automobile, was revealed yesterday to be the man who killed his first wife of 1926.

Mr. Nesbitt, who operated a delicatessen at 2037 Madison Rd., O'Bryonville, had never told his wife, Mrs. Beatrice Nesbitt, that he killed his first wife in their Troy, Ohio, home in one of Ohio's most noted murder cases.

He had married his present wife 11 years ago. They have a son, seven years old.

Mr. Nesbitt confessed to the late Ora Slater, famed Cincinnati private detective, that he killed his wife in a fit of rage after a series of quarrels. He was sentenced to the Ohio Penitentiary and was released in 1935.

Mrs. Beatrice Nesbitt was amazed at this revelation.

"It couldn't be the same man," she said. "He never told me. He was a wonderful man. He couldn't have been more tender. He was liked by everyone."

A friend in Troy, Ohio, who heard the widow's words, added: "He really was liked by everyone and was a nice fellow. His first wife nagged him until – as he said when he finally confessed – he saw "red" and bashed in her skull at their home."

This story was written by Kermit W. Vandivier and co-written by Roxanne Gross

www.ingramcontent.com/pod-product-compliance
Ingram Content Group UK Ltd.
Pitfield, Milton Keynes, MK11 3LW, UK
UKHW051133260726
13967UKWH00010B/3025

9 781105 892936